Autumn

Library of Congress Number: 80-25190

2 3 4 5 6 7 8 9 0 85 84 83

Printed in the United States of America.

Library of Congress Cataloging in Publication Data

Allington, Richard L
 Autumn.

 (Beginning to learn about)
 SUMMARY: Introduces the reader to various activities
traditionally associated with autumn and encourages the
discussion of individual experiences.
 1. Autumn — Juvenile literature. [1. Autumn]
I. Krull, Kathleen, joint author. II. Bond, Bruce.
III. Title. IV. Series.
QB631.A387   500   80-25190
ISBN 0-8172-1343-0

Richard L. Allington is Associate Professor, Department of Reading,
State University of New York at Albany.
Kathleen Krull is the author of twenty-five books for children.

BEGINNING TO LEARN ABOUT

AUTUMN

BY RICHARD L. ALLINGTON, PH.D., • AND KATHLEEN KRULL

ILLUSTRATED BY BRUCE BOND

Raintree Childrens Books • Milwaukee • Toronto • Melbourne • London

There are four seasons in a year.

spring

summer

autumn

winter

Each season lasts about three months.
In many places, autumn is the season
when leaves fall from the trees.
Autumn is also called "fall."

Autumn comes after summer.
Winter comes after autumn.
Which picture shows autumn?

I see things that tell me autumn is coming.
The days are warm, but the nights are cool.
Many fruits and vegetables are ready
to be picked.

What signs tell *you* that autumn is coming?

Where I live, autumn is
the time of big storms
called hurricanes.

What special weather do *you*
have in autumn?

Where I live, school starts in the autumn.
The wind blows the leaves down from
the trees.

What special things happen during autumn
where you live?

Where I live, we play
basketball in the autumn.

What other autumn sports
can you think of?

I hear special sounds in autumn. Leaves
crackle. The wind seems to moan.
Nuts drop from the trees.

What sounds do you hear during autumn?

As the weather gets colder, I wear warmer
clothes — a jacket, and maybe a scarf.

What special clothes do you wear in autumn?
Why?

Autumn brings special feelings. Seeing the leaves change color makes me feel happy. But sometimes I wish that summer would come back.

What special feelings do you have in autumn?

In the autumn, I like to pick berries.
Sometimes I save leaves by pressing
them into big books.

What do you like to do in autumn?

In autumn I sometimes see
shadows that look like
ghosts — especially on
nights when the moon
is full.

What special things do you
see in autumn?

Where I live, autumn is the best time of year to taste fresh fruits and vegetables.

What special things do you eat in autumn?

During autumn, the animals get ready for winter. Birds fly south. Squirrels hide enough nuts to last the whole winter.

What do other animals do to get ready for winter?

I see things that tell me autumn is ending
and winter is coming. The trees are bare.
Puddles freeze over. The days get shorter.
Sometimes it snows.

What signs tell you that autumn is ending?

Say the names of the twelve months in the year.
Which months are the autumn months?

January

February

March

April

May

June

July

August

September

October

November

December

Draw a picture, using autumn colors
(such as red, orange, yellow, brown).
Write or tell someone a story about the picture.

APR 7 '06			

World Faiths

CHRISTIANITY

Alan Brown

Chrysalis Education

WORLD FAITHS

BUDDHISM   CHRISTIANITY
HINDUISM   ISLAM
JUDAISM   SIKHISM

Produced by Bender Richardson White, PO Box 266,
Uxbridge UB9 5NX

Distributed in the United States by
Smart Apple Media
1980 Lookout Drive, North Mankato, Minnesota 56003

ISBN 1-59389-131-8

The Library of Congress control number 2003105003

Editorial Manager: Joyce Bentley   Senior Editor: Sarah Nunn
Project Editor: Lionel Bender   Text Editor: Peter Harrison
Designer: Richard Johnson   Art Editor: Ben White
Proofreader: Jennifer Smart   Production: Kim Richardson
Picture Researchers: Joanne O'Brien at Circa Photo Library, and Cathy Stastny
Cover Make-up: Mike Pilley, Radius   Maps and Diagrams: Stefan Chabluk

Thanks to Joanne O'Brien at ICOREC, Manchester, for planning the structure and content
of these books.

Picture Acknowledgments
We wish to thank the following individuals and organizations for their help and assistance, and for
supplying material in their collections: Circa Photo Library: pages 5 top, 6, 8, 13, 14, 20, 22, 23, 24,
25, 40, 46; cover, 1, 9, 34, 37 (John Smith); 3, 48–49, 52–53 (William Holtby); 5 center 11, 12, 15, 35
(Christine Osborne); 5 bottom, 18, 33, 50–51 (Danny Fitzpatrick); 17, 19, 54–55 (Zbigniew Kosc); 21,
26, 31 (John Fryer); 41 (Martin Palmer); 42 (Bipin J. Mistry). Corbis Images: 29 (Bob Krist), 30 (Steve
Raymer); 32 (Earl & Nazima Kowall); 43 (DiMaggio/Kalish); 44 (Tom Nebbia); 45 (Lester
Lefkowitz); 47 (Corbis Images Inc.). Lionheart Books: 38. Topham Photo Library: 4 (The Image
Works/Esbin-Anderson); 7 (The Image Works); 10 (Picturepoint); 27 (Picturepoint); 28 (Associated
Press). The pictures used in this book do not show the actual people named in the case studies in
the text.

CONTENTS

Anne-Marie's Story

Anne-Marie is 15 years old and lives with her two sisters and one brother in Birmingham, England. She is the eldest child in her family, so her Mom and Dad expect her to help look after her brother and sisters. Her family is Roman Catholic, and she goes to a Roman Catholic secondary school.

"CHRISTIANITY IS AN important part of my life. I go to church on Sundays and really enjoy the youth club at the church during the week. At the moment, we are organizing a summer fair, where we will raise money to buy a sound system for use at the club.

My school is a strong support for me in my faith. When I am there I help prepare for the Mass, and I have special responsibilities in the school for organizing worship. Both my church and my school provide me with good guidance for my future life, but the strongest influence is my family.

In everything we do, we focus on the events of the life of Jesus Christ. One thing we learn that is important to me is that I am a member of a worldwide community with 1000 million members. My school has contacts with Catholic schools in other parts of the world, and one adventure coming up soon is the chance to visit a school and family in Italy. This means I will be able to visit Rome and go to the Vatican, where the Pope – the leader of the Roman Catholic Church – lives.

At home I help my younger brother, Declan, prepare for his First Communion. For Roman Catholic children, this is when we become part of this enormous Church. His First Communion will be the first time he can fully join in the Mass where bread and wine is shared – the most important service in the church. He will receive a wafer and wine that we believe is the body and blood of Jesus. Declan will look very smart in his white shirt and best clothes. I will soon confirm the promises made at my baptism at my Confirmation in a couple of years' time

I am also thinking about my trip to Lourdes. My church has organized a trip to Lourdes in France where St. Bernadette had a vision of Mary, the mother of Jesus. Our Lady, as we call her, is an important person for Catholics. Lourdes, where people go to be healed, to pray, and to worship, is a place of pilgrimage for Catholics.

My trip will reinforce my faith, which guides me to make the right choices when I face difficult issues."

Christians across the world

Christianity has over 2000 million followers, of which 50 percent are Roman Catholic.

INDIA
Christians make up 2 percent of the Indian population. Tradition says Christianity was brought to India by Thomas, one of Jesus' disciples. Here they celebrate St. Thomas' Day, carrying banners through the streets in Kerala.

SOUTH KOREA
Young Christians at a Roman Catholic church in Seoul. South Korea. Christianity – as well as the Muslim faith – is growing fast throughout Asia, where there are many Buddhists, Hindus, and Sikhs. This causes some religious conflict.

SOUTH AMERICA
A procession of a figure of the Virgin Mary and baby Jesus honors a local saint's day in Nicaragua. Brought to South America from Europe in the sixteenth century, Christianity is now the main religion in the region.

What Do Christians Believe?

Christians believe Jesus Christ is God's son, their Savior. He was born and lived a human life in the Middle East about 2000 years ago. He was killed by the authorities, but rose from the dead, and he saves those who follow him from sin, allowing them to live with God forever.

CHRISTIANS BELIEVE IN the teachings of Jesus Christ. Jesus was a teacher and preacher who grew up in Galilee, now part of Israel. Jesus said he had come to teach the true meaning of the religious teachings of the Jews, that had been given to the Jewish people over many centuries.

Jesus taught that all the rules and teachings about how to live could be summed up in a few short sentences: "Listen, Israel! The Lord your God is the only Lord. Love the Lord your God with all your heart, with all your soul, with all your mind, and with all your strength."

The Ten Commandments

Given to the Jewish leader, Moses, about 1400 years before Jesus, they form the basis of Jewish law and much of modern Western morality:

- there is only one God;
- the seventh day is special;
- parents should be honored;
- people should not worship idols;

it is forbidden to:

- steal;
- murder;
- commit adultery;
- bear false witness (lie);
- swear using God's name;
- want other people's possessions.

This South African painting shows the loving heart of Jesus, and his open arms welcoming people to him.

Christians believe it is important to be kind to one another, help each other, and respect other people's views.

His second most important message was: "Love your neighbor as yourself. From this commandment follow all the law and the prophets." Jesus tried to show people how important it was to follow God's teachings. The religious authorities disapproved of Jesus' teachings, and within three years of starting to preach, he was put to death.

Who was Jesus?

Jesus of Nazareth, c.6 B.C.E.–32 C.E., is the most important figure in the Christian religion. He was born into a Jewish family and his father was a carpenter. When he was about 30 years old he began to teach and preach. Jesus angered the religious authorities because he claimed to do things only God could do. He claimed to forgive people's wrongdoings – their sins or offences against God.

Seen as a threat to the community, Jesus was sentenced to death. Christians believe that three days after he was crucified (executed on a cross), Jesus rose from the dead and is alive today. This makes the life of Jesus very special.

DEBATE - Is Jesus' rule, love your neighbor as yourself, relevant today?

- Yes. If we all loved and respected others we would never deliberately harm them.
- No. Today's problems are too complex to be solved in such a simple way. We need new rules and attitudes for the twenty-first century.

Was Jesus the son of God?

Christians believe Jesus fulfilled all the promises made to the Jewish people over the centuries. They believe he showed God's love for the world. He called God "Father" and taught his disciples a prayer starting "Our Father." The Gospels – the accounts of the life of Jesus – tell of a voice coming from heaven saying, "This is my beloved son in whom I am well pleased."

Christians gather in groups to pray, read from the Bible, and reflect on Jesus' teachings and their relevance to everyday life.

What does "Christ" mean?

Christians believe that Jesus was the Christ. The word "christ" comes from a Greek word, *christos,* which, in turn, is a translation of the Hebrew word, messiah. The Jews believe that the Messiah or "Anointed One" – the leader chosen by God – will come one day to bring about the rule of God on Earth. It will be a time of justice, peace, and harmony. Christians believe that Jesus is the Anointed One, the person promised by God.

What do Christians mean by "salvation?"

Christianity is a religion of salvation – deliverance from the power and effects of sin. It teaches that human beings have disobeyed the commands God gave to the Jewish people, and broken their promises to obey God's will. There are many rules that the Jewish people were required to keep, the best known being the Ten Commandments. In breaking these laws, people became separated from God. Christians believe that Jesus' life and death mended that relationship.

Those who listened to Jesus' teaching and believed in him would enter into a new and special relationship with God. Their wrongdoings or sins (offences against God) would be forgiven and they would be reunited with God in heaven.

How did Jesus teach?

Jesus taught that the time had come for God's kingdom to be fully accepted throughout the world. He taught in four ways: by speaking to people; by using stories (parables); by using miracles; and through the example of his life, death, and resurrection.

Jesus wanted people to come back to God and follow his teaching. He asked people to accept God into their lives and obey God's teachings. He hoped that people would learn by listening to him speak and by watching his actions. If people would follow his example, they would be following God's will. As soon as they accepted his message, they need have no more fears or worries, because God would look after them.

Services, such as this one in a Roman Catholic Church, offer Christians regular opportunities to hear Jesus' teachings and interpretations of their meanings.

A parable

Parables were a form of teaching used by the Jews of Jesus' time. The rabbis – Jewish spiritual leaders – used stories from everyday life to entertain and teach.

This is one of Jesus' parables: *The kingdom of God is like a mustard seed, which a man took and sowed in his field. As a seed, mustard is smaller than any other; but when it has grown, it is bigger than any garden-plant; it becomes a tree, big enough for birds to come and roost among its branches.*

How did Jesus get people to listen?

Jesus' parables were captivating. A parable is a story that has layers of meanings. It can be simply enjoyed and remembered as a good story, easily memorized for retelling or thinking about later. Jesus' parables encouraged listeners to think of new interpretations as their faith grew. Some parables were long stories, others were just a few sentences long. Almost all of them were taken from everyday situations that the people living at the time would have been able to relate to. They gave meaning to people's lives.

Did Jesus perform miracles?

Jesus used miracles to teach. Miracles were not new in the Jewish tradition; they were signs of the power of God. The Jewish scriptures have many stories about individuals being healed or even brought back from the dead. There are stories of Jesus stilling a storm when his disciples were afraid, and of healing a paralyzed man after telling him his sins were forgiven.

Jesus used miracles as a demonstration of God's power. There have been many healers before, during, and since Jesus' time. Today many Christians claim to use the power of Jesus to heal, and some people do seem to have been healed. What Jesus claimed was that he had the power to forgive sins. Some of his healings imply that the person's illness was caused by the sinful acts of that person. So by curing the illness, Jesus was forgiving the person's sins. The Jewish authorities, however, believed Jesus' claim was blasphemy (an offence against God), punishable by death, because only God could forgive sins.

DEBATE - Can a person be human and divine?

* Yes. God's power is infinite so he can do things that are beyond our understanding.

* No. If a person was divine they wouldn't truly experience the fears and temptations of ordinary human beings.

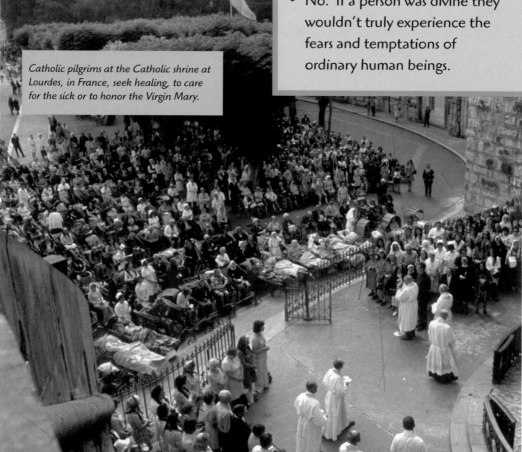

Catholic pilgrims at the Catholic shrine at Lourdes, in France, seek healing, to care for the sick or to honor the Virgin Mary.

What were the motives for his miracles?

Jesus did not heal people only out of compassion or pity. He may have cured only a small percentage of sick or disabled people living around him. Jesus healed to speak about himself and the power of God. People had to understand who and what Jesus was. Jesus healed blind people and deaf people as a sign that those who listened to him would see and hear what he taught. "Look," "listen," and "understand" are important words in the Gospel stories of Jesus.

Was Jesus divine?

Christians believe there is, and only ever has been, one God. However, they refer to God in three ways: as the Father Creator; as the Son, Jesus Christ; and as the Holy Spirit, the power of God that people feel and experience in their lives.

So Christians talk about God as Father, Son, and Holy Spirit , or the Trinity – three in one. For Christians, the idea of Father, Son, and Holy Spirit – the Trinity – expresses the principal ways God and human beings interact with each other.

The Lord's Prayer

When his disciples asked Jesus how they should pray, he gave them this prayer: *Our Father, who art in heaven, thy name be hallowed, thy kingdom come. Thy will be done, on Earth as in Heaven. Give us today our daily bread. Forgive us the wrong we have done, as we have forgiven those who have wronged us. And do not bring us to the test, but deliver us from evil.*

A Christian service, celebrating the life of Jesus, is held outside, on a housing estate in London. Communual services do not have to be held in a church.

What Were The Origins Of Christianity?

Christianity developed in Galilee, in Israel, 2000 years ago as a result of people's faith in Jesus rising from the dead. For Christians, it is who Jesus is that lies at the heart of the Christian faith, not just what he taught.

PANEM SCIFICAT XPC Qy O SECVLA PASCAT.
ABLVIT EXTERIVS SORDES Qy COB LAVAT INTVS.

IN ALL THE Gospels, the last week of Jesus' life is given the greatest importance. For Christians, it is what Jesus does in the last week of his life that makes him so special. They believe he rose from the dead.

What was Jesus' life like?

Very little is known of the first 30 years of Jesus' life. Most of the information given in the Christian Gospels focuses on what he said and did in the last three years before he was crucified. There is no contemporary external evidence at all of Jesus' life.

Stained glass windows and illustrations, like this one from Romania from about 1750, often tell Bible stories because for centuries few people could read. Here, Jesus shares his last meal with his disciples (top), before which he washed their feet (below).

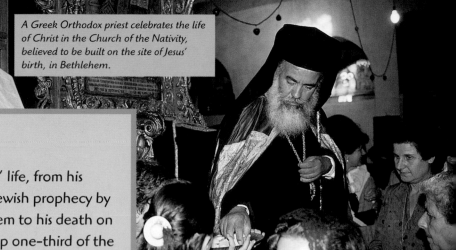

A Greek Orthodox priest celebrates the life of Christ in the Church of the Nativity, believed to be built on the site of Jesus' birth, in Bethlehem.

Holy Week

The end of Jesus' life, from his fulfilment of a Jewish prophecy by entering Jerusalem to his death on the cross, take up one-third of the accounts of his life in the Gospels. Those events are celebrated by Christians in the week before Easter, which they call Holy Week.

Matthew and Luke say in their Gospels that Jesus was born in Bethlehem, near Jerusalem, and grew up with Joseph, his father, and Mary, his mother, in Nazareth in Galilee. When Jesus was about 30 years old he was baptized by John the Baptist (a relative) and this marked the beginning of his teaching life. Jesus traveled throughout Judea – roughly the area of modern Israel – teaching and healing. He gathered together 12 men around him, known as his "disciples, who followed him wherever he taught."

Why was Jesus arrested and crucified?

Jesus was a Jew and often taught in synagogues. His teaching followed the traditional Jewish style of religious debate and its content would be very familiar to those who listened to him. The main concern of many Jews who heard Jesus was that he appeared to claim to forgive sins. The Gospels tell of conflicts between Jesus and the Jewish authorities in Jerusalem. He was arrested, tried by the Jews, and then by the Roman governor, Pontius Pilate.

Pilate could find no evidence against him, but the people of Jerusalem demanded his execution.

How did Jesus spend his last days?

The Gospels tell of Jesus entering Jerusalem on a donkey a week before his death, fulfilling the Jewish scripture that the Savior of Israel would come on a beast of burden. To enter Jerusalem on a horse would resemble a conquering king; to enter on a donkey was a symbol of humility. Crowds welcomed him then, waving palm branches, throwing them before him and shouting: "Hosanna to the Son of David! Blessings on him who comes in the name of the Lord!"

On the night before he was arrested, Jesus ate a meal with his 12 disciples, celebrating the Jewish festival of Passover. He asked them to remember him when they broke bread and drank wine together, saying: "Do this in remembrance of me." He told them that one of the disciples sitting with them and sharing the meal would betray him to the authorities, and that Peter, his chief disciple, would three times deny knowing him. Both predictions came true, and the meal became known as the Last Supper.

Christians believe Jesus was taken up into heaven forty days after he rose from the dead.

The disappearance

Two Gospels say women followers of Jesus were first to find the grave stone removed and Jesus' body gone. They told the disciples what had happened. At first the disciples would not believe the women. Then Peter and John, two disciples, rushed to the grave to verify what the women had told them. Under Jewish law of the time, women were not allowed to be witnesses in court, so it was important their story was verified by men.

Crucifixion was a common Roman method of execution: they crucified thousands of people. Jesus' death on the cross was confirmed by stabbing his side with a spear. His body was taken down, wrapped in a sheet, and placed in a grave cut out of rock. A heavy stone was rolled over the opening.

How did Jesus die?

Jesus was flogged, then made to carry a heavy, wooden cross through the streets of Jerusalem. When he reached the top of the Hill of Calvary, his hands and feet were nailed to the cross, and he was left to die hanging between two criminals.

Why is Jesus' resurrection so important?

For Christians, the most special events of Jesus' life were his birth, death, and resurrection (rising from the dead). They believe that God sent his only son, Jesus, to share in what it means to be a human being. Jesus was so obedient to God's

wishes that he was prepared to die an agonizing death. Because he did what God asked, he rose from the dead and others who followed him would also live forever with God in heaven. Most Christians believe that Jesus rising from the dead is literally true, an historical fact. Others believe it is a way of describing how powerfully his followers felt him to be with them after his death

What did the early Christians believe?

The first followers of Jesus were Jews who had heard him teach. Soon, Gentiles (non-Jews) came to "The Way" (an early name for Christianity). They had heard about it from Jesus' followers and wanted to be baptized. What did they actually believe? Statements of belief, or "creeds," arose as people joined Jesus' followers. They put aside previous beliefs and were "washed clean." They believed Jesus was the Messiah who made it possible for everyone to live with God forever.

A female priest holds up the bread and wine, symbols of Jesus' body and blood, at Holy Communion.

DEBATE – Can someone really rise from the dead?

- Yes. Patients have "died" during operations but revived. Some say they speak to dead people at séances. Jesus' resurrection proves he was the Son of God.

- No. No one can prove resurrection. There are logical explanations for speaking with the dead and why Jesus' body had gone from the grave.

How Did Christianity Develop?

Jesus' followers thought that, after the crucifixion, the end of the world would soon come, fulfilling Jewish prophecies. When it did not, they began to write and teach Jesus' message.

PEOPLE WHO WANTED to become Christians had to learn about Jesus and find the relevance of his teaching to their lives. The most effective way of doing this was to listen to the Bible being read and the teaching of the Church.

The Christians' Bible is made up of the Old Testament, scriptures handed down from the Jewish religion, and the New Testament, written in the first century after Jesus' death. The word "testament" means promise, and Christians believe that God's promises to human beings are contained in the Bible.

What is in the New Testament?

The New Testament includes the Gospels, other books, and a number of letters to Christians written by early teachers such as St. Paul. One book, The Acts of the Apostles, gives an account of the disciples just after the death of Jesus. Another, The Revelation of St. John, looks toward the end of time.

There are four Gospels, named after the men who wrote them: Matthew, Mark, Luke, and John. Each tells the life of Jesus. The four were probably Christians writing between 30 and 60 years after Jesus died, not Jesus' closest followers.

Rosaries, most often used nowadays by Roman Catholics to focus their thoughts when praying, were first used by Eastern Christian monks in the third century C.E.. Similar kinds of beads are used by Buddhists, Hindus, and Muslims.

The Gospels do, however, reflect the teaching and beliefs of the first disciples.

Who was Paul and why is he important?

Paul was a tentmaker from Tarsus in present-day Turkey. He was a very learned Jew. He was originally called Saul and became a persecutor of early Christians. He tells how he watched the persecution of Christians by the authorities. One day while traveling to

Jesus in the Bible

The Old Testament contains 39 books and the New Testament 27. The Gospels are episodes from the life of Jesus passed on verbally before being written down. Christians believe the Old Testament tells of the coming of their savior; the New Testament shows how all the Old Testament prophecies were fulfilled in Jesus.

Damascus to persecute Christians, he had a vision of Jesus, who asked him to stop threatening his followers. So stunned was Saul that he changed his name to Paul and spent the rest of his life writing, teaching, and preaching about Jesus. He traveled around the Middle East, writing letters that are now in the New Testament, before being taken to Rome, where he probably died in about 65 C.E.

Paul is important to Christians for several reasons. First, he was converted to Christianity in a very personal way – by Jesus speaking to him directly. Second, he wrote letters helping people to understand Jesus' teaching, and giving guidance on Christian behavior that is still relevant today. Third, he persuaded Jesus' followers that new converts did not have to become Jews and follow Jewish laws before they became Christian. This meant that non-Jews would find it easier to accept Jesus' teaching. It meant that very soon most Christians would not be Jewish at all, unlike Jesus and the first disciples.

How did early Christianity spread?

Jesus' followers were Jews but over about 30 years it became clear that many non-Jews also wanted to become Christians. Paul went out to the Gentiles to preach about Jesus and they saw the relevance of his message. There was hostility from Jews who did not accept this new teaching, and eventually they excluded the Christians from their synagogues (places of worship). The Christians then had to set up their own networks.

Tradition says one disciple, Thomas, went to India and others traveled in the Mediterranean area. Paul gave energy and drive to early Christian missionary work, however. He went to Turkey, Greece, and eventually to Rome.

As Christianity spread, it became necessary for Christians to become organized. Groups gathered under the authority of a bishop. In the first century after Jesus' death, people were given roles of responsibility in the new faith, such as elders and deacons. They began to organize the new religion. These roles were to be developed much more in the following centuries.

What did this new religion believe?

Entry into The Way was by baptism. Jesus had been baptized at the beginning of his ministry and Christians wanted to be "washed clean" of their past life. New Christians would say they believed Jesus was Lord, that there was One God, Father, Son, and Holy Spirit, and that Jesus had risen from the dead.

Paul wrote in one of his letters: "If there is no resurrection, then Christ was not raised; and if Christ·was not raised, then our Gospel is null and void, as is your faith." So to state belief in Jesus rising from the dead was, and is, the key

Secret signs

For their first 300 years, Christians were persecuted by the Romans. They chose secret signs to recognize each other, such as the fish. The letters of the Greek word for fish – *ichthus* – stood for the words: Jesus Christ God's Son Savior. Other signs were the boat and the anchor.

A monk blesses a child outside a church in Bolivia. Christianity was spread rapidly through South America by sixteenth–century Spanish and Portuguese explorers and missionaries.

commitment for Christians. This belief would be revealed in the way that Christians would treat each other. They believed that as God had shown his love by sending his son, Jesus, to Earth, they should show their love for God by loving each other. The early Church shared all their possessions, food, and life together.

DEBATE – Should we question the truth of religious books such as the Bible?

- Yes. Some situations are complex. If we question the Bible our knowledge will advance and humankind will move forward, even though dealing with change may be difficult at times.

- No. Some books are true for all time, the Bible is one of them and answers all our present concerns. We need to distinguish the Bible from books that only reflect what is happening now.

The Mount of Olives in Jerusalem, in "the Holy Land." This is a sacred burial place for Jews, the site of Jesus' crucifixion and resurrection – marked by the Catholic and Orthodox churches seen here – as well as the location of the Dome of the Rock, an important Muslim mosque.

Are All Forms Of Christianity The Same?

To be a Christian is to believe Jesus Christ is your Lord and Savior. So why are there so many different Churches? How can Christians be so divided when the message of Jesus is so clear?

BEING A CHRISTIAN is not just reading the Bible or going to church. While most Christians do these things regularly, they also believe that every person should be treated as if they were Jesus. He taught that if someone helps the poor, the needy, and the outcast, then it is as if they are helping Jesus personally. This can be very demanding but it does not mean one has to be polite or well-mannered all the time. Indeed, sometimes one may have to get angry or forceful to ensure that the poor receive their due support.

How should Christians behave?

Christians believe each person should be treated as if God were in them. A person

Churches, like this one in Kenya, produce and sell a wide variety of religious publications. Money to produce these usually comes from charitable donations or fundraising events.

People choose to do it freely because of their concern, or love, for those in need.

In Christianity, "charity" was established in one of the letters of Paul, written to the people of Corinth in Greece. In this he wrote that there are three things that last forever: faith, hope, and charity (or love), but the greatest of these is charity. Paul may have written those words 2000 years ago but they guide people's actions today, and not just those of Christians. The concept of charity and love has now become fundamental to Christianity. As a result, many Christians take part in charitable activities. Also, while Christianity has had difficult periods, it has done a great deal of good work through creating schools, hospitals, and other charitable organizations to help those in greatest need.

may disagree with another person's beliefs or think that their actions are wrong, but as a Christian they should never give up on that person because God never gives up on them. It is the wrongdoing that is loathed, not the person: "The sin not the sinner."

Christians try to find out from God how they should behave in different situations. They do this in four main ways. They will read the Bible, pray to God for guidance, listen carefully to their Church, and look at the example of Jesus. There is the golden rule: "Do to others as you would have them do to you," or "Love your neighbor as yourself." This helps Christians decide how to meet the various decisions they have to make in their lifetime.

Do all Christians believe in charity?

Charity, a form of love, is the most important characteristic of the Christian faith and all Christians try to practice it in their daily lives. Charity involves helping those less fortunate than oneself in a variety of ways. Sometimes people give money. At other times, they give their time. Often, they give both, but charity is always a voluntary action.

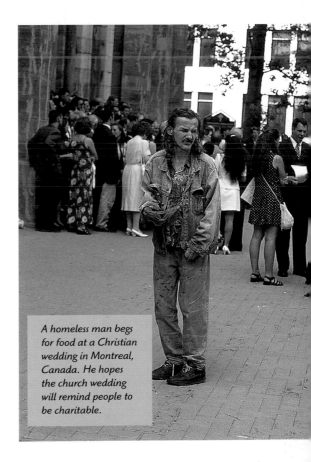

A homeless man begs for food at a Christian wedding in Montreal, Canada. He hopes the church wedding will remind people to be charitable.

What is the "Church?"

Christians use the word "church" in four main ways. It can mean the building in which Christians meet to worship. It can refer to the people who worship in that building – the congregation. It can mean the members of a branch of Christianity, such as the Roman Catholic Church or the Methodist Church. It can also mean Christians throughout the world – all the followers of Jesus Christ (in these last two cases it is usually spelt with a capital "C".)

There are four main branches of Christianity, all of which are spread across the world. The branches are: the Roman Catholic Church, the Orthodox Churches, the Protestant Churches, and the Pentecostal Churches.

What defines the types of Christianity?

The beliefs of the Churches are very similar. They all believe in Jesus Christ and accept the basic creeds of Christianity agreed hundreds of years ago. The differences are mainly those of worship and of the authority of the

Church, and many reflect the culture and environment of the followers. So the differences are mainly of interpretation and what has grown up around the Churches over the centuries. It is rather like a family in which there will be much agreement and acceptance of differences with the occasional argument that needs to be settled with tact and sympathy.

Church building

Christians did not build churches for 300 years after the death of Jesus because of persecution by the Romans. Only when Constantine became Emperor of the Roman Empire and accepted Christianity did the Christians feel safe enough to build houses of worship.

The U.S.A. has a large church-going community. The answer of these Christian people to the problems of the world is easy to see.

A Greek Orthodox Priest in robes in a church in Crete.

Church design

Most Orthodox churches do not have seats (neither did many older Roman Catholic churches when they were built). In Orthodox churches, the floor represents the world and the ceiling, heaven. Large images of Jesus painted on the ceiling look down on the worshipers. Such a picture of Jesus is called the pantocrator (Creator of All) and represents Jesus as Creator and Judge of the World.

What are the oldest Churches?

The Roman Catholic and the Orthodox Churches are the two oldest. As Christianity grew during the first 1000 years, there arose some differences between the Orthodox Churches and the Church in Rome. Eventually, in 1054, they agreed to go their separate ways, although in recent times there has been much closer cooperation between them.

The Roman Catholic Church has its headquarters in the Vatican in Rome and claims Peter, Jesus' chief disciple, to have been its first bishop. The head of this Church is the Pope. All the priests are unmarried because they are "married" to the Church.

The Orthodox Churches take their name from "orthodox," meaning true worship. They have four Patriarchs as their head priests rather than one person. While their priests can be married, the bishops and senior clergy may not. Many Orthodox Churches are named after the country where they were formed: there are Syrian Orthodox; Russian Orthodox; Greek Orthodox Churches, and so on.

The World Council of Churches adopted this symbol of a boat with a cross as a mast. The Greek word oikoumene (meaning "one house") is the root of the English word ecumenical, used to describe the united Christian Churches working together.

What defines the Protestant Churches?

The Protestant Churches generally trace their origins to the sixteenth century, when there arose a great "protest" about abuses in the Roman Catholic Church. People such as the German, Martin Luther – a Roman Catholic monk – and the Frenchman, John Calvin, led opposition to the Roman Catholic Church. It was a time of upheaval in Europe. The invention of the printing press made the Bible more available and there was social unrest. The time was ripe for a change.

Over the next century or so, such Protestant Churches as the Lutheran, Reformed, Presbyterian, and Baptist were established, followed later by the Quakers – the Religious Society of Friends – the Methodists, and the Salvation Army. In the 1530s, the Church of England – the Anglican Church – broke from the Church in Rome over the unwillingness of the Pope to accept the divorce of the English king, Henry VIII. As this Church took shape, it retained many Catholic practices in worship but adopted many Protestant attitudes, too. For this reason, the Church of England is often regarded as a bridge between the Roman and Protestant Churches.

Lutheran Church

Martin Luther was a German monk. He nailed his religious objections to the door of Wittenberg church before eventually leaving the Roman Catholic Church and getting married. His main objection was to "indulgences" – offering forgiveness of sins in return for money. The Church that bears his name is popular in Scandinavia, Germany, and the U.S.A.

What defines Pentecostal Churches?

The Pentecostal Churches developed in the black communities of the U.S.A. at the beginning of the twentieth century. Mainstream Churches were unable to meet the needs of this deprived and oppressed group. A movement arose taking the name "Pentecost," in remembrance of the time when the Holy Spirit was given to Jesus' disciples. Pentecostal Churches believe the Spirit of God gives them power to heal and preach the Gospels. They are noted for their powerful singing and emotional services.

Who leads worship?

Different churches have services led in various ways by people with a range of titles and roles. Some are called priests, some ministers; some are married, some are not; some have women priests and ministers, others do not. In some Pentecostal Churches they are called "pastors" because they care for the people. The word "pastor" comes from a Greek word meaning one who cares for a flock.

Some Pentecostal Churches have women ministers, as do many Protestant Churches, but they still prefer a man to be the pastor of their flock, just as the Orthodox and Roman Catholic Churches do. The reasons for this are that Jesus chose only male disciples and Paul, in his letter to the people of Corinth, writes that women should not address the congregation. Some modern churchgoers might disagree with Paul on this point.

DEBATE – Should there be freedom of choice?

There are so many sorts of Christian Churches, believers can pick the one they like. Is it good to have a large number of alternative kinds of worship to choose from?

- Yes. People are more likely to attend church and take part in the community if they are able to attend the one that most suits their personality and beliefs.

- No. All the Christian churches worship the same God and have the same basic principles, therefore you should stay with the same church as your family so that you can worship together.

Pentecostal Church communities, like this New Testament Church of God, are lively centers, with services including powerful singing and praying.

How Do Christians Celebrate Their Faith?

Christians celebrate their faith not only by going to church, reading the Bible, and marking the main events of the Christian year in festivals and fasts. They also express their beliefs through bringing up their children in the faith and marrying in church. Some Christians are ordained as priests or ministers.

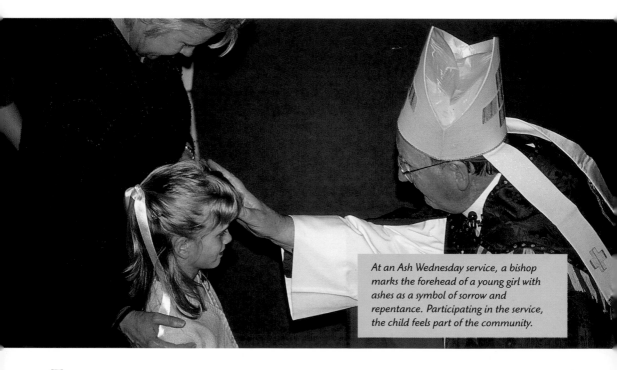

At an Ash Wednesday service, a bishop marks the forehead of a young girl with ashes as a symbol of sorrow and repentance. Participating in the service, the child feels part of the community.

ALL CHRISTIANS WANT to mark important times in their life by re-affirming and re-dedicating their lives to God. The important moments surround birth, entry into adulthood, marriage, and death. They are called "rites of passage" because they mark the transition when a person moves from one stage to another.

What does Baptism mean?

Baptism is the outward sign that the person has become a Christian, that he or she has joined the Church. Jesus was baptized by his cousin, John, when he began his ministry, so virtually all Christians will be baptized at the start of their own Christian journey. Putting water on the forehead, or going down under the water and then rising up, is done to symbolize the washing away of past wrongdoing, and being reborn as a follower of Jesus Christ.

When is baptism performed?

The first Christians were baptized as adults but, as time went by, parents wanted babies to be accepted as well. The older Churches – the Roman Catholic and Orthodox – baptize babies, as do the Anglican churches. Traditional churches use a font and pour water over the baby's head. The Orthodox Churches make sure that the baby is entirely immersed. By contrast, some of the Protestant Churches believe that people cannot become full members of the Church before they are old enough to make promises for themselves. So the Baptist Church, for example, baptizes adults in a baptistery – a pool laid in the floor of the church building.

What does it mean to be confirmed?

Confirmation is an event in which Christians confirm their religious beliefs. When a baby is baptized, the godparents and parents make promises to be a good Christian on behalf of the child. When the child is older, he or she will be able to confirm those vows for themselves. People being confirmed will have taken some instruction in the faith to make sure they are fully aware of their commitment and that they are doing it with free will. Confirmation usually takes place in front of a bishop, who places his or her hands on the person's head, blesses them, and receives them into full membership of the Church. Confirmation can take place from the age of about 10 onwards.

Open-air baptism

In the early Church, Baptism had to take place in moving water to make visible the movement of the Holy Spirit in human life. This is why today, in warmer countries, Baptism often takes place outdoors in flowing rivers and streams.

A Pentecostal baptism of an adult in the River Jordan, Israel.

Pope John Paul II, leader of the Roman
Catholic Church, blesses people after the
Mass on Christmas Day, from the balcony
of St. Peter's Cathedral in the Vatican,
Rome, in 1996.

What is Holy Communion?

At Jesus' last meal with his disciples
before he was crucified, he asked them
to remember him whenever they ate
bread and drank wine together. Nearly
every Christian group celebrates this
event by communing, or sharing, bread
and wine, though they carry out this
church service in different ways. The
bread is the body of Jesus Christ and the
wine his blood.

The Roman Catholic Church and the
Orthodox Churches believe that in some
mysterious way the bread and wine
actually become Jesus' body and blood
at Communion. Most other Churches
believe Holy Communion is a very
special memorial meal that Christians
keep to remember the sacrifice of Jesus.

What are the Mass and Eucharist?

Roman Catholics call Holy Communion
the Mass. It may be because the last
words of the church service in Latin are
Ite, missa est, meaning "Go, the mass is
ended." Anglicans call the service the
Eucharist, from the Greek for
"thanksgiving." The Last Supper, or The
Lord's Supper, are common names
among Protestant Churches. Anglicans
vary in use between these names. In all
cases there are readings from the Bible
and a sermon or address.

What is First Communion?

There is, in the Roman Catholic Church, an important ceremony when a child is about 8 years old. He or she is allowed to receive the bread and wine – his or her first Holy Communion. The child is dressed in fine clothes for the ceremony – a girl in a white dress, a boy in a white shirt, perhaps a tie, and dark trousers. First Communion marks a middle stage between Baptism and Confirmation.

A First Communion group in Georgetown, Guyana.

Communion without wine

The Salvation Army and the Quakers are the two best-known Christian groups that do not celebrate Holy Communion. Other groups, such as the Methodists, use non-alcoholic wine in the ceremony as a statement about the perils of alcohol.

What happens at a Christian wedding?

For all Christian couples, the most important aspect of the ceremony is that the bride and bridegroom make their promises before God. The details of the ceremony vary greatly, depending on the Church and the wishes of the couple and their families.

It is not known whether Jesus was married or not, but one of the Gospels describes him attending a wedding and that passage is often read out at the service. The wedding is a uniting of two people, body and soul, in the presence of friends and relatives and before God. The couple exchange promises of faithfulness, and to love and support each other whatever the future brings. Marriage is for mutual support and the upbringing of children, and prayers are offered on behalf of the couple. Some couples have a Mass, called a Nuptial Mass, at the service, or have a Communion service during which they re-affirm their commitment to Christ.

A Roman Catholic bride and groom at their wedding in Vietnam.

Divorce

Roman Catholic teaching states:
*The intimate union of marriage...
demands total fidelity from the
spouses and requires an unbreakable
unity between them.*
Divorce is not recognized in the
Roman Catholic Church, but is
permissible in other Churches.
Some of these Churches will, under
certain conditions, allow divorced
people to enter into a new
marriage in a church.

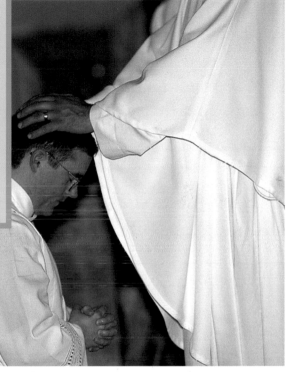

*Some Christians believe God has called them to be
priests or ministers. In this church a priest is ordained by
the Bishop laying hands on him and giving him the
authority to be a priest.*

What are the Sacraments?

A dictionary defines a sacrament as an
oath of allegiance, an obligation, or a
formal religious act as a sign of belief. In
the Christian Church, there are usually
recognized to be seven sacraments.
However, many Protestant Churches do
not recognize all of them. The seven are:
Baptism and Holy Communion as the
major sacraments Jesus participated in;
then Confirmation, Marriage,
Confession, Healing, and Ordination.
They are all outward signs that God is
with the believer.

Confession is the opportunity to confess,
or own up to, one's sins to God. Sinners
tell their sins to a priest (their confessor),
who listens in confidence on God's
behalf. Penitents must speak honestly
and be truly sorry if they are to be given
absolution (be released from
responsibility). Finally, penitents are
given a penance by the confessor, which
is often the saying of specified prayers,
to atone for their wrongdoings.

Ordination is the appointment of a
person as a preacher or authority in the
Church. Some people believe they are
called by God to be priests or ministers.
If the Church considers a person
suitable, they begin training before being
ordained in a special ceremony. The new
minister will then work under someone
with more experience for a time.

What are the "last rites?"

These are prayers usually said by a priest from the Roman Catholic Church in the presence of a dying person. They are prayers that ask God for forgiveness and ensure that the dying person's sins are forgiven before he or she dies and, as Christians believe, enters the presence of God. The sign of the cross is made on their forehead, mouth, and chest.

What is the Christian view of death?

Christians believe that when Jesus comes again they will rise from the dead. This is why, traditionally, Christians are buried, not cremated. In fact, the Orthodox Churches do not allow cremation. Funerals can be very sad times, especially for those who have a relative or a close friend who has died. Some Christians, however, see funerals as a joyous occasion for they are certain that the dead person has gone to heaven to live with God forever. They have not died; spiritually they have moved on to be with God and to begin a new and better life.

Most church funeral services include prayers and a short talk about the dead person before burial in the churchyard or cemetery. Gravestones in churchyards are usually put up several weeks after a burial to allow the ground to settle. There are rules and regulations about the design of the headstone and what can be written on it; these vary with each Church and individual priest or vicar.

A burial procession at a cemetery in India. The graves are adorned with flowers.

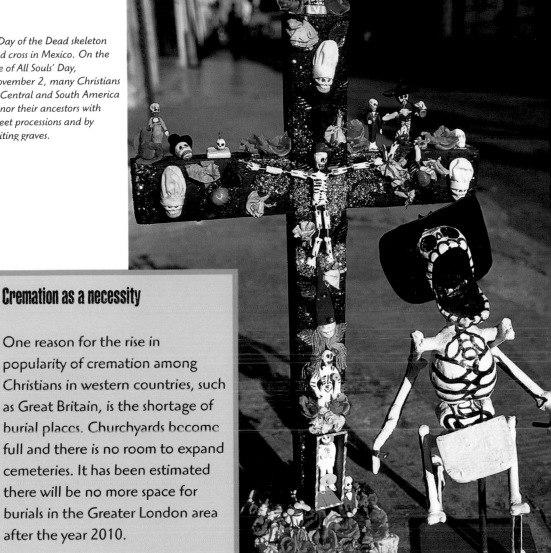

A Day of the Dead skeleton and cross in Mexico. On the eve of All Souls' Day, November 2, many Christians in Central and South America honor their ancestors with street processions and by visiting graves.

Cremation as a necessity

One reason for the rise in popularity of cremation among Christians in western countries, such as Great Britain, is the shortage of burial places. Churchyards become full and there is no room to expand cemeteries. It has been estimated there will be no more space for burials in the Greater London area after the year 2010.

Flowers are laid on the grave as a symbol of life. They are a mark of respect, and on a place of burial indicate the dead person is not forgotten.

If the person is to be cremated, there will be a short service called a "committal" at the crematorium. After the cremation, the ashes are given to the family. They may be interred – buried or placed in a cask or urn – or scattered in a place or places that are particularly connected with the deceased.

What is a memorial service?

In some cases, a memorial service is held as well as, or instead of, a funeral. This usually only happens when the person who died was particularly famous or if their body was lost or buried far from home. The service is held at a time and place that allows as many people as possible to attend. The structure of the service is agreed between the priest and the person's family and close friends. It is a time of thankfulness and of remembering the life of the dead person.

An Easter procession in Manchester, England. The procession from the church, led by the Salvation Army Band, takes the cross of Jesus through the streets. The Salvation Army is known throughout the world for its charitable work with the poor and the destitute, as well as for the music of its brass bands.

What festivals do Christians celebrate?

Most holy days in the Christian calendar commemorate the events in the life of Jesus and the beginning of Christian faith. The main festivals – Easter and Christmas – are celebrated by all Churches. Others, such as Saints' days and harvest festivals, are celebrated by some and not others. Most festivals are celebrated in church, but they also have an important place in home life, too.

What is Easter and how is it celebrated?

Easter is a time when Christians remember the events surrounding the crucifixion, death, and resurrection of Jesus. It comes after a time of preparation called Lent, when many Christians give up luxuries in memory of when Jesus spent 40 days fasting and praying in the desert before he started teaching. Children and adults may give up sweets and chocolate for Lent, and families will enjoy resisting temptation. They will also say prayers and read their Bibles more regularly. The start of Lent is remembered in families as Shrove Tuesday, or Pancake Day, when all fatty

Jesus' birthday

Christians did not celebrate the birth of Jesus for 300 years after his death. The specific date chosen – 25 December – was known as the Festival of the Unconquered Sun in the Roman calendar. The first Nativity scene is believed to have been created by St. Francis of Assisi, in Italy, a monk of the early thirteenth century, noted for his love of Jesus and animals.

foods in the home are used up. In some countries, Mardi Gras – French for "Fat Tuesday" – is a great street festival.

Holy Week includes Easter itself. The week starts on Palm Sunday, when Jesus entered Jerusalem. Maundy Thursday marks the Last Supper. Jesus was crucified on Good Friday – so-called because Jesus willingly sacrificed himself and God helped human suffering. Jesus rose up from the dead on Easter Sunday. At Easter there are services in church for families to attend and there are special times at home:

Christmas Day celebrations on a beach in Queensland, Australia. Santa Claus represents St. Nicholas, a Christian saint who, according to tradition, looks after children. Today Christian children receive presents from him on Christmas Day.

cards, good wishes and, for some, the excitement of getting up early to watch for the dawn on Easter Day, with the joy of saying "Christ is risen."

What happens at Christmas?

Christmas celebrates the birth of Jesus. Families come together and people send one another Christmas cards to maintain long-standing friendships. Leading up to Christmas there are Nativity plays when the events of the birth of Jesus are acted out, and carol services when songs of praise are sung, and the story of Jesus' birth is read. At Christmas itself there are services in churches. Great efforts are made to ensure the homeless and the destitute have a place to go where they can be fed and kept warm.

The Bible stories of Jesus' birth tell of local shepherds being told by angels of this great event. They go to a manger, or animal stall, where they find the newborn child. Twelve days later, three Wise Men guided by a star also arrive at the manger, to worship Jesus, and bring him gifts. All Christians celebrate this story and for up to 12 days after Christmas, festival lights and decorations adorn homes and streets.

How Do Christians Worship?

Christianity is a community religion. Christians join together to worship God and pray to him. There are Christians who go to church regularly, others who go occasionally at festival times, and others who never go.

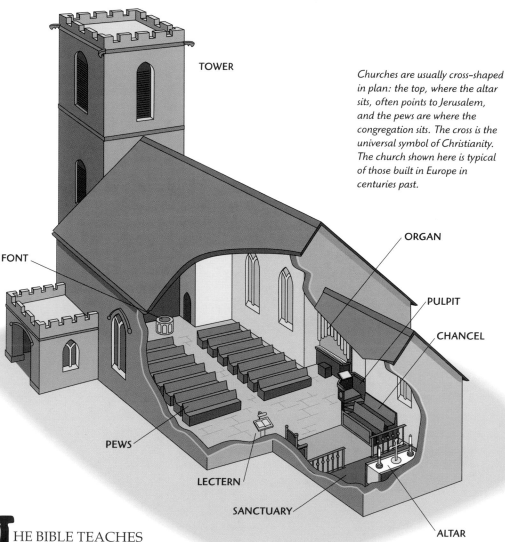

TOWER

Churches are usually cross-shaped in plan: the top, where the altar sits, often points to Jerusalem, and the pews are where the congregation sits. The cross is the universal symbol of Christianity. The church shown here is typical of those built in Europe in centuries past.

FONT

ORGAN

PULPIT

CHANCEL

PEWS

LECTERN

SANCTUARY

ALTAR

THE BIBLE TEACHES Christians that Jesus was concerned about people. Although some Christians do worship on their own, for most it is important to share the faith with others and to join together in what is often called "fellowship." It is part of Christian life to enjoy the company of

Christian parents often encourage their children to join in church services to help them form their own relationship with God.

Bible translations

The Bible's original languages were Hebrew and Greek, but it has been translated into nearly all known languages. Christians often study the Bible using prepared notes that explain the text and show how the Bible is relevant in their lives.

other Christians, who will share many of one's views on current issues and be helpful and supportive of one another.

Some Christians will go to church every day. Others will go once a week and more often during special times in the Church's year. Christians have their main worship on Sunday because that was the day Jesus rose from the dead.

What happens in church?

There are regular services in which people sing, listen to teachings, say their prayers, confess their wrongdoings to God, and give God thanks for the good things in life.

Most services follow a set order, though the Pentecostal Churches tend to be more relaxed about time and order. Holy

Communion is the most important service in the Orthodox, Anglican, and Roman Catholic Churches. In many churches, there are children's services and midweek meetings for prayer or social groups. For many, churchgoing is for reflection, a time to think about their lives and their relationship with God. They may be in difficult times, or have hard decisions to make and feel the need to talk to God about them. Church services, or the quiet peaceful atmosphere and the support of other Christians, can give people the time and space to do so.

How is the Bible used in church?

The Bible will be read during most services. Usually there are readings from the Old and New Testaments, especially from the Gospels. In some churches, the Bible is carried into the church before it is read and the congregation stands when the Gospel is read. Because Christians believe the Bible is God's word, it has to be treated with reverence and care. The congregants listen carefully to the readings and try to apply what they hear to their own lives.

How do Christians worship at home?

Families have different customs. Some will "say grace," giving thanks to God before or after a meal. Others will read the Bible together or tell stories from it. Parents often say prayers with their children when they go to bed, and there may be Christian signs and symbols, such as crucifixes, throughout the home. Some Christian homes will have a family Bible handed down from generation to generation. It may not be read very often but it is a sign of the strong Christian tradition in the family. Other families will do all these things.

Why do Christians read the Bible?

When Christians read about Jesus, they try to use their imagination so they can share, to some extent, in his experiences.

On Good Friday, Christians may walk through a town, as they do in Jerusalem, carrying a cross as Jesus is described as doing on the way to his crucifixion. In churches on Good Friday there will be vigils during which people imagine they are at the foot of the cross watching Jesus die, sharing his pain and that of his disciples. On Easter Sunday, Christians believe that the lighting of candles shares in Jesus – the Light of the World – rising from the dead. In these ways, Christians act out the story of Easter.

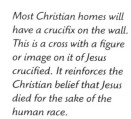

Most Christian homes will have a crucifix on the wall. This is a cross with a figure or image on it of Jesus crucified. It reinforces the Christian belief that Jesus died for the sake of the human race.

Different stories

The four Gospels tell of different events. When Matthew's Gospel talks about Jesus' birth, it mentions a plot by Herod to kill Jesus. Luke talks about Mary, and tells of the shepherds' visit to the baby. The single message for Christians at Christmas is the love of God.

Quiet, personal study of the Bible is important for all Christians. It allows them to deepen their understanding of the Bible's message, and to strengthen their own relationship with the written word of God.

Many Christians visit Israel so they can walk in the regions where Jesus walked, sail in the Sea of Galilee, look at sites where Jesus may have visited, and pray in the Church of the Holy Sepulchre, built on the site where Jesus was supposed to have been buried.

What does the Bible say?

The Bible is the Christian handbook for life. It contains examples of how one should live one's life and there are rules and guidance. The Bible is a collection of human experiences. There are stories of individuals who have not always managed to do God's will all the time – just like many people today – but are nonetheless good men and women.

For Christians the Bible is a book that supports and gives direction to every member of the family.

DEBATE – Should the Bible be open to new interpretation?

Some people argue that holy books such as the Bible that come from a certain period in history should be reinterpreted to make more sense to today's readers

* Yes. If these books are to be relevant to us, they need to address the problems of today.

* No. They were inspired by God and some people believe they are the actual words of God, so they cannot be changed. We must make greater efforts to study what God was asking of us and then put it into practice.

How Does Christianity Deal With Modern Issues?

Christianity has had to change for more than 2000 years while still remaining true to its basic teaching. Christians have to apply the teaching of Jesus to situations that were unknown or not thought of centuries ago. They can and do, on occasion, arrive at different conclusions.

THERE ARE FIVE main sources of authority and guidance for Christians. The first place they look is the Bible, to see what direct guidance it can give. Secondly, sometimes there is no direct answer, and Christians must reflect on and interpret the Bible text in relation to their own situation. Thirdly, there is the authority of the particular Church the Christian belongs to. Some Churches have very clear and firm guidance on specific issues. Others leave greater responsibility on the Christian to speak with God in private prayer, which is the fourth authority. The fifth authoritative guide is tradition: the customs and practices associated with Christian teaching down the ages. These sources mean that while there may be differences in the advice given on specific subjects, the Christian will find support and guidance.

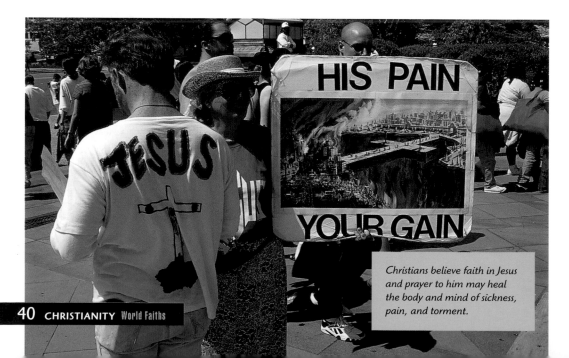

HIS PAIN

YOUR GAIN

Christians believe faith in Jesus and prayer to him may heal the body and mind of sickness, pain, and torment.

A war memorial in Washington D.C., U.S.A., to soldiers of the Vietnam War. Creating and visiting memorials help the healing process.

Why is forgiveness a Christian value?

Just as charity comes from the love of God, so Christians believe that if a person wants God to forgive his or her own wrongdoing, then he or she has to be ready to forgive those who do wrong to them. Jesus, Christians believe, had the power to forgive sins or wrongdoing against God. Even on the cross at his crucifixion he asked God to forgive those responsible because they did not know what they were doing. Jesus' teaching says that forgiveness is important, but for God to forgive a person, he or she has to forgive as well.

Forgiveness is not easy, and when one does wrong it is important to be truly sorry for one's actions and thoughts. Christians believe that, if a person tries not to repeat a wrongdoing, God will forgive him or her. Peter asked Jesus how many times he should forgive someone – seven? Jesus replied "Seventy times seven," meaning unlimited times as long as that person is genuinely sorry, God will then forgive them likewise.

DEBATE - Should you forgive and forget?

- Yes. One has to trust people and believe they can improve. Make sure they understand their wrongdoings and how hurtful they have been. If they show remorse, be full of forgiveness.

- No. People play on forgiveness as a soft option. They will keep on doing bad things knowing they will be forgiven and are able to avoid punishment all the time. If, after a few times of forgiveness, they do not improve, they should not be given another chance.

How important is charity for Christians?

One of the most important things Christians can do is care for others. They believe that God loved the world so much that he sacrificed his son, Jesus, so they in turn should be prepared to do the same with their lives for God. This means that many Christians are involved in charities. Some work for Christian charities, such as Christian Aid, while others help small local charities, or work with neighbors who need help and support. In recent times, Mother Teresa, famous for her work in the slums of Calcutta, founded the Roman Catholic Order of the Sisters of Charity to help the very poorest people.

Mother Teresa's order of nuns works with homeless and exploited people in the poorest areas of the world.

Christian groups like the Salvation Army are devoted to helping the poor and homeless. While they hope to convert people to the Christian faith, their main activity is to serve and tend those in greatest need regardless of their religion.

Some Christians give one-tenth of their income to charity; this is called tithing. Others give their time and energy to the needy. Charity is a way of living their faith. Some Christians prefer acting out their commitment to Jesus in this way rather than going to church regularly.

Can women be priests?

Churches differ on this issue. There are already women ministers in many Protestant Churches. The Church of England, like most of the other Anglican churches, allowed women to be priests in 1992 but they are not allowed to be bishops; it was, and still is, divided over the issue. As yet there are no women priests in the Roman Catholic or Orthodox Churches. These two groups resist women priests because Jesus chose only male disciples.

Rules can change, however. Peter, the first Bishop of Rome, was married, not celibate, so there was an exception right from the start of Christianity. To change the rules so the Orthodox and Roman Catholics agreed would mean there would have to be one great Council of the Churches, and that is unlikely to happen as they are fiercely autonomous.

What is the view on homosexuality?

Relying on Biblical texts, Christians are generally opposed to homosexual practice. Recent research has suggested that homosexuality may be genetic or decided by early experiences in life.

Some Christians believe sexual activity should only take place in the sanctity of

Christianity is still debating the ethics of homosexuality.

marriage. While many are sympathetic to people who are homosexual, they believe these individuals should not have sexual relations. Rather, they should be celibate and accept their situation. Other, more liberal Christians, feel this is an unreasonable request. There is a vigorous and unfinished debate among Christians about attitudes to homosexuality and whether homosexuals may be ordained as clergy.

What is the Christian attitude to abortion?

One of the main bases of the Christian faith is that God created the world and everything in it. God creates life and only God has the right to take it away. Christian teaching is opposed to abortion, although some churches do allow exceptions. Clearest of all is the Roman Catholic Church, which opposes abortion in all cases. Most other Churches also reject abortion but accept there may be exceptional circumstances, such as when the health of the mother is at risk. It is also partly a question of when life is believed to have begun. If it begins at the moment of conception, then any abortion can be regarded as the taking of life, but some scientists and clergy define life as beginning sometime after conception.

Is contraception acceptable?

The Roman Catholic Church believes in the sanctity of all life. It is up to God to decide whether sexual intercourse should result in a child being conceived.

The couple may not therefore use any artificial means to stop conception, for that is to take on the power of God to make decisions. There are, of course, couples who do practice contraception, and the Roman Catholic Church has been under pressure to agree to the use of condoms to reduce the risk of A.I.D.S.

Other Churches have less decided attitudes on these topics, and while

Making a choice

The Church of England General Synod – a council of all branches of the Anglican Church – has stated that: *Christians need to face frankly the fact that in an imperfect world the "right" choice is sometimes the lesser of two evils.*

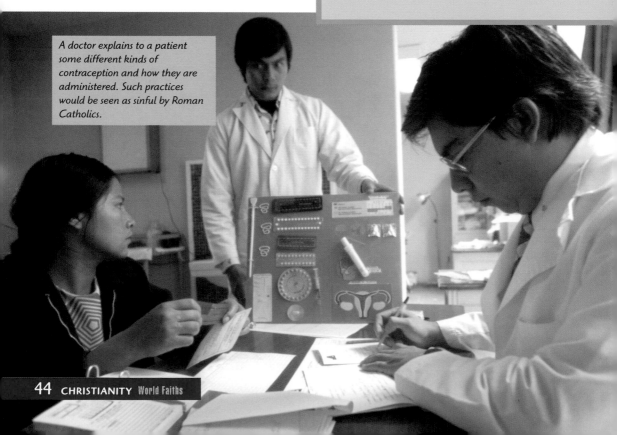

A doctor explains to a patient some different kinds of contraception and how they are administered. Such practices would be seen as sinful by Roman Catholics.

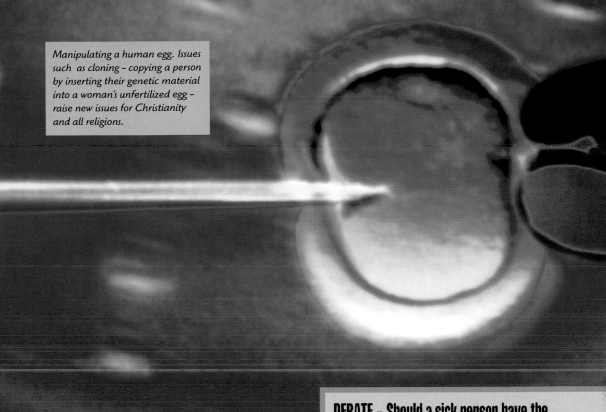

Manipulating a human egg. Issues such as cloning – copying a person by inserting their genetic material into a woman's unfertilized egg – raise new issues for Christianity and all religions.

some Protestant groups may have similar views to the Catholic Church, most regard contraception as a private matter of conscience. Genetic engineering is something to be watched very carefully before making a final decision because the consequences could be enormous.

Do Christians allow euthanasia?

The short answer is: No, because God gives life and God takes it away. Euthanasia is often known as "mercy killing" – helping hopelessly sick people to die peacefully and painlessly. All the Churches are opposed to euthanasia as they believe the process could be abused. While a person's suffering may be intolerable, the Church's view is that it can produce love and care in those who tend for them and that this life is not the end; there is another life where the suffering person will live again in peace with God.

DEBATE – Should a sick person have the right to end his or her own life?

- Yes. People should have the right to die when they want. It is cruel to keep them alive when they are in great pain or have no dignity. They are no longer the people they were.

- No. Everyone has a life to live and it is not over until God decides. If God has given life, God will decide whether he or she will be rewarded in the next life. One cannot just avoid certain aspects of life even if one does not like them. People must go through all that life offers.

What does the Bible teach about creation?

The Bible teaches that God created the world out of a formless void. The stories of creation show God being the architect of creation but giving human beings responsibility and stewardship over that creation. Creation is inspired by God's power, his spirit, but human beings have a concern to care for the world and for all of creation.

Many Christians feel that there is no contradiction between these Bible stories and evolution, while others take the stories literally and do not believe in evolution at all. It seems reasonable that Christians can interpret creation as they wish, as long as they do not deny the place of God. Christian teaching says that God is the creator and his Holy Spirit maintains life; the details are up to the different churches or to individual Christians to interpret themselves.

A multifaith celebration of religion and creation at Winchester Cathedral, England. In recent years, Christian Churches have worked hard to establish an understanding and rapport with other faiths, and to make a commitment to the conservation of the environment.

Why is there a rise in fundamentalism?

Scientists have made much progress in understanding the world during the last 2500 years. They have not had all the answers, however, and some scientific knowledge has been misused, causing such problems as increased pollution and the threat of misuse of nuclear energy. These problems have left people feeling unsure of the future and in need of the security provided by a faith. Christianity is a faith offering a clear promise of a place in heaven. This may be why fundamentalist churches, with strict rules and literal interpretations of the Bible, have increased in popularity recently, especially in the United States. These churches provide a close-knit community and clear guidelines for their members.

Believers and non-believers

- Fundamentalist Christians calculate from the Bible that creation took place c.8000 years ago.

- 40 percent of citizens in the U.S.A. attend church regularly compared to about 10 percent in the UK.

World leaders commemorate the 11 September 2001 terrorist attack on the World Trade Center twin towers in New York, U.S.A. People's inhumanity to one another and the suffering it causes continues.

Why does God not stop all the suffering?

Christians would say "only God knows." They believe in a God who came to Earth and experienced the painful events of everyday living, plus extraordinary agony on the cross when he died. This means that Christianity has a suffering savior at its heart. Jesus did not take away his suffering but told God he would be obedient to God's will. He is an example to Christians that whatever happens they need faith in God.

Christians try to help those who suffer by undertaking charitable work; they have founded hospitals and schools, as well as organizations to support the poor and destitute. Ill health and natural disasters, for example, are reminders of the impermanence of life and that only faith in God brings security and the hope of a better life with God after death.

Debate - Should one country interfere in the running of another country?

Much religious teaching is about the importance of caring for others.

- Yes. If people in a country are being badly treated by its government or regime, then it is the duty of other countries to step in and try and change things for the good of all.

- No. It is wrong for one country to assume it knows best and to interfere in the running of another country — unless that country's people have asked for help or that country is a threat to world peace.

REFERENCE

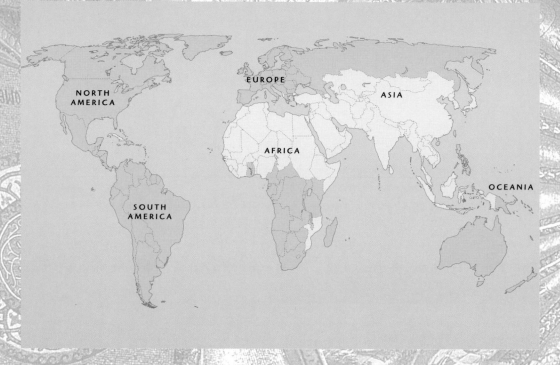

Christians around the world

There are over 2000 million Christians in the world. Half of them are Roman Catholic of which 50 percent live in Central and South America; the majority of Christians today are non-white and live in the southern hemisphere. No country in the world, however, does not have at least a few Christians in it.

There are over 22 000 different Christian groups or sects. Christianity is growing fast in Africa: the number of Christians in 1950 was 25 million; by 1980 it was 100 million; and by 2000 it was more than 200 million.

In England and Wales there are 44 648 registered or recorded places of Christian worship. Of these, as recorded at the Registrar General's office in 1999: 16 464 were Anglican; 3708 were Roman Catholic; 3332 were Baptist; 7576 were Methodist; 1752 were United Reformed; 1377 were Congregationalist; 944 were Salvation Army; 949 were Brethren; and 365 were Quakers (The Religious Society of Friends). There are no totals kept in the Registrar General's office for the Orthodox Churches, Lutherans, the various Pentecostal churches or the House churches.

Timeline of Christianity

Before the Common Era (B.C.E.)
c.6–4   Birth of Jesus.

Common Era (C.E.)
c.29–33 Crucifixion of Jesus.
50   Council of Jerusalem. Agreed Christians should not keep Jewish law.
60–100 The four Gospels probably written.
c.62   Death of Peter, Jesus' leading disciple and first Bishop of Rome.
c.65   Death of St. Paul.
64–300 Period of persecution of Christians by Romans after fire destroys part of Rome. Christians blamed.
70   Destruction of the Temple in Jerusalem.
84   Christians excluded from synagogues.
200+   Arrival of Christianity in Britain; development of Celtic Christianity.
300+   Christians begin church building.
325   Council of Nicea.
382   Contents of the Christian Bible agreed.
c.540   Benedict draws up rule for monastic movement.
597   Augustine arrives in Britain "to bring English people back to Christianity." Beginning of struggle between Roman and Celtic forms of Christianity.
1054   Separation of Roman Catholic Christianity from Orthodox Churches of the East.
1096   First Crusade begins to recapture Christian sites in Palestine from Muslims.
1170   Thomas Becket, Archbishop of Canterbury, murdered in Canterbury Cathedral.
1209   Francis of Assisi founds Franciscan Order of monks.
1215   Dominican Order of monks founded by Dominic.
1517   Martin Luther posts his 95 Theses on church door in Wittenberg – heralding the start of the Reformation.
1534   Act of Supremacy recognizes Henry VIII as Head of English Church.
1536   John Calvin publishes his *Institutes*.
1611   King James I Authorized Version of the Bible is published.
1633   *Mayflower* sails to America to found colony guaranteeing religious freedom.
1642   George Fox starts the Religious Society of Friends (Quakers).
1738   John and Charles Wesley found the Methodist movement.
1822   Joseph Smith receives vision leading to foundation of Mormons.
1868–70 First Vatican Council passes decree of Papal infallibility.
1878   Salvation Army founded by William Booth.
1910   Ecumenical beginnings of Christian Churches at Edinburgh Missionary Conference.
1948   Foundation of World Council of Churches.
1948   Mother Teresa founds Order of the Missionaries of Charity.
1960   John F. Kennedy is the first Roman Catholic to be voted President of the U.S.A.
1962–65 Second Vatican Council brings changes to the Roman Catholic Church such as services no longer in Latin.
1966   Cultural Revolution closes all Christian churches in China.

The Six Major Faiths

BUDDHISM
Founded
535 B.C.E. in Northern India

Number of followers
Estimated at 360 million

Holy Places
Bodh Gaya, Sarnath, both in northern India

Holy Books
The Tripitaka

Holy Symbol
Eight-spoked wheel

JUDAISM
Founded
In what is now Israel, around 2000 B.C.E.

Number of followers
Around 14 million religious Jews

Holy Places
Jerusalem, especially the Western Wall

Holy Books
The Torah

Holy Symbol
Seven-branched menorah (candle stand)

CHRISTIANITY
Founded
Around 30 C.E., Jerusalem

Number of followers
Just under 2000 million

Holy Places
Jerusalem and other sites associated with the life of Jesus

Holy Books
The Bible (Old and New Testament)

Holy Symbol
Cross

HINDUISM
Founded
Developed gradually in prehistoric times

Number of followers
Around 850 million

Holy Places
River Ganges, especially at Varanasi (Benares). Several other places in India

Holy Books
Vedas, Upanishads, Mahabharata, Ramayana

Holy Symbol
Aum

SIKHISM
Founded
Northwest India, fifteenth century C.E.

Number of followers
16 million

Holy Places
Amritsar

Holy Books
The Guru Granth Sahib

Holy Symbol
Nishan Sahib: swords and a circle

ISLAM
Founded
610 C.E. in Arabia (modern Saudi Arabia).

Number of followers
Over 1000 million

Holy Places
Makkah and Madinah, in Saudi Arabia

Holy Books
The Qur'an

Holy Symbol
Crescent and star

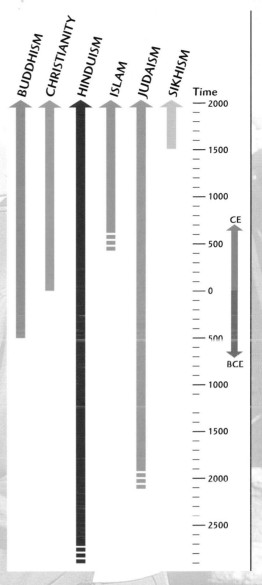

While some faiths can point to a definite time and person for their origin, others can not. For example, Muslims teach that the beliefs of Islam predate Muhammad and go back to the beginning of the world. Hinduism apparently developed from several different prehistoric religious traditions.

GLOSSARY

Absolution God's forgiveness after a Confession.

ascend Go up or rise.

baptism A ceremony where a person joins the Christian Church. It involves the sprinkling or pouring of water on to a person's forehead or immersing the whole body in water.

Baptist A person who baptizes someone. Also, a member of the Baptist Church and/or a person who believes only adults should be baptized.

B.C.E. Before the Common Era.

blasphemy Disrespectful talk about God or sacred things.

C.E. Common Era.

census An official count of people in a population.

Christ The Anointed One: often called "Messiah" from the Hebrew.

church A Christian organization; a building used for Christian worship; the people worshiping in the building; or all Christians worldwide.

Confession The formal admission of one's wrongdoings or sins, often to a priest.

Confirmation The act of confirming the promises to follow the Christian faith that were made at one's baptism.

creed A formal statement of Christian belief.

crucified Put to death by being nailed or bound to a cross. Roman method of execution.

denomination A branch of Christianity, for example the Roman Catholic Church.

disciple Someone who followed Jesus during his life. A follower or pupil of a teacher.

Epistle A letter.

Eucharist The central act of Christian worship, the sharing of bread and wine to share in the life of the risen Jesus Christ. Also known as Holy Communion , the Lord's Supper, or the Mass.

Gentiles The name given to non-Jews by the Jews.

Gospel Meaning "Good news." One of the four books in the Bible that tell us about Jesus' life.

holy Concerned with God or religion, something "sacred."

Holy Week The seven days leading up to Easter Sunday.

Kingdom of God (Heaven) The place where God rules; a place of peace where people live together with God. Jesus taught a lot about the Kingdom of God being present if people only listened to his teaching.

Lent The period of 40 days (not including Sundays) of fasting and repentance leading up to Easter.

Messiah The long awaited Anointed One of God who would right all wrongs and bring about the Kingdom, or rule, of God on Earth.

ministry Work with, and spiritual service to, other people.

miracle An extraordinary and welcome event that cannot be explained by the laws of nature or science.

Orthodox Traditional Christianity (or other faith) which requires strict observance of commandments, beliefs, and customs.

Parables Stories with levels of meanings used to make a point. A lot of Jesus' teaching took the form of parables.

Pentecostalism The twentieth-century movement stressing the gifts of the Holy Spirit, such as healing and preaching.

pilgrim Someone who travels to a holy place for religious reasons.

Pope The Bishop of Rome; the leader of the Roman Catholic Church.

prophet Someone who speaks for God and tells people what God wants.

Protestant The branch of Christianity that split from the Roman Catholic Church during the Reformation in the sixteenth century.

religious Concerned with or believing in a religion.

Resurrection Jesus' rising from the dead.

Roman Catholic The branch of Christianity that has as its leader the Pope based in the Vatican in Rome.

Sabbath The Jewish weekly holy day. It begins before sunset on Friday and ends at nightfall on Saturday.

Sacrament A sign of the presence of Jesus Christ. The seven sacraments are: Baptism; Confirmation; Holy Communion; Confession; Marriage; Ordination, and Healing.

sacrifice Give up something precious, including one's own life.

sermon A religious talk.

sin Going against God's wishes. Something separating a person from God.

soul The spiritual part of a person.

synagogue A building where Jewish people meet, pray, and study.

Temple The building in Jerusalem that was the center of Jewish religious life at the time of Jesus. Destroyed by the Romans in 70 CE.

Testament Another word for "promise." The Bible consists of the Old Testament (the witness of the Jewish prophets) and the New Testament (the witness of Jesus' life and times).

Trinity The presence of Three Persons (Father, Son, and Holy Spirit) in one God.

worship Honor God, usually by prayer, singing hymns, reading psalms.

FURTHER INFORMATION

Books to read
Jesus and Christianity by Alan Brown (Wayland, 2002).

The Christian World by Alan Brown (Macdonald Young Books, 1996).

Festivals: Looking at Christianity by A. Seaman and G. Owen (Wayland, 1998).

Jesus and Mary by A. Seaman and G. Owen (Wayland, 1998).

Worship by A. Seaman and G. Owen (Wayland, 1998).

Christians 'Through the Ages' Round the World by John Drane (Lion Publishing, 1999).

Christianity: Ideas Bank RE by E. McCreery (Folens, 1995).

Christianity: Photopack RE by D. Rose (Folens, 1995).

Living Religions: Christianity Part 1 by C. Richards (Nelson, 1996).

Stories from the Christian World by D. Self (Macdonald Young Books, 1998).

Teaching about Jesus by A. Ewens and M. K. Stone (RMEP, 2001).

The Jesus Story by M. Batchelor (Lion Publishing, 1995).

Teaching Christianity by L. Weatherley and T. Reader (CHP/National Society, 2001).

Videos
Life Stories Channel 4
Jesus of Nazareth Channel 5
StoryKeepers Paternoster
God's Story – New Testament Yorkshire Television

CD ROMs
Conflict in Jerusalem: Jesus' Last Days Lion Publishing
Risen Jesus: The Week that Changed History Lion Publishing
Lion CD of the Bible and Christianity Lion Publishing
Lion PC Bible Handbook Lion Publishing

Web addresses
www.christianteens.about.com
Website with information on various subjects, as well as a bookstore.

www.christiansunite.com
Includes many links on subjects such as recreation, church history, summer camps and books.

www.crosssearch.com
PDI is a movement of 45 local Chrstian churches in the U.S., Mexico, Canada, and the U.K.

Organizations

Christian Coalition of America
P.O. Box 37030
Washington D.C. 20013-7030

Catholic Charities
1731 King Street
Alexandria, VA 22314

Everything Christian
1375 Myrtle Avenue
Cincinatti, Ohio 45209

Canadian Council of Christian Charities
1-21 Howard Avenue
Elmira, Ontario
Canada N38 2C9

GEMS Girl's Clubs
P.O. Box 7259
Grand Rapids, MI 49510

World Council of Independent Christian Churches
P.O. Box 406
Harpers Ferry, WV 25425

The Christian Media Network
P.O. Box 448
Jacksonville, OR 97530

Mid-Atlantic Christian Education
Association
P.O. Box 5433
Concord, NC 28027

INDEX